AQA REVISION

GCSE 9–1
AN INSPECTOR
CALLS

BY J.B. PRIESTLEY

GREAT ANSWERS

T0382074

SCHOLASTIC

Published in the UK by Scholastic, 2024

Scholastic Education, Bosworth Avenue, Warwick, CV34 6UQ

SCHOLASTIC and associated logos are trademarks and/or registered trademarks of Scholastic Inc.

© Scholastic, 2024

2 3 4 5 6 7 8 9   4 5 6 7 8 9 0 1 2 3

A CIP catalogue record for this book is available from the British Library.

ISBN 978-0702-33171-8

Printed and bound by Bell & Bain Ltd, Glasgow

The book is made of materials from well-managed, FSC®-certified forests and other controlled sources.

Due to the nature of the web we cannot guarantee the content or links of any site mentioned.

We strongly recommend that teachers check websites before using them in the classroom.

Every effort has been made to trace copyright holders for the works reproduced in this book, and the Publishers apologise for any inadvertent omissions.

www.scholastic.co.uk

For safety or quality concerns:
UK: www.scholastic.co.uk/productinformation
EU: www.scholastic.ie/productinformation

Author
Rob Pollard

Editorial team
Rachel Morgan, Vicki Yates, Caroline Lowe, Julia Roberts and Laura Stannard

Typesetting
Jayne Rawlings/Oxford Raw Design

Design team
Dipa Mistry and Andrea Lewis

Illustrations
Jim Eldridge

Photograph
page 31: An Inspector Calls set, Ruth Neeman

Contents

About this book

This book is designed to demonstrate what a great answer for your AQA GCSE English Literature exam on *An Inspector Calls* (Paper 2, Section A) looks like. It demonstrates a step-by step process from first sight of the question through to a full answer. The process shows you how to approach each step, from analysing what the question is asking you to do, to planning your answer, showing how it meets the assessment objectives for the exam paper and finally presenting a great answer and an examiners response. All the answers in this book have been written in the light of advice from examiners and using tips drawn from the examiners' reports over the last few years.

It is important to note that one question can give rise to multiple different great answers. What these great answers all have in common is that they are based on an excellent interpretation with sound exploration of the evidence. Great answers are not *right* answers, they are rich and well-argued answers.

In this book you will find the following features that will help you understand how to achieve that all-important great answer in your exam.

Zoom in on the question

How does Priestley explore ideas about guilt in *An Inspector Calls*

Write about:

- the ideas about guilt in *An Inspector Calls*
- how Priestley presents these ideas by the way he writes.

Consider the play as a whole and how it relates to the time is was written and performed. (AO3)

Consider what parts of the play relate to this theme and what Priestley wants the audience to think. (AO1)

Keep focused on the **language** and dramatic methods Priestley uses to influence the audience. (AO2)

Analysis of the question to help you focus on what the question is actually asking you.

Ideas to help you cover the AOs for each question and matching colour-coded commentary within the answers to show you how these are achieved.

AO1
Mr and Mrs Birling's refusal to accept their guilt.Sheila's guilt at having Eva fired/Eric's guilt at having abused her/Gerald's ambiguous response/the Inspector's role in uncovering the guilt of the Birlings.

AO2
Analysis of the differences between **characters** and how this is shown through their speech and action.
Mr Birling: 'a man has to…look after himself.'
Mrs Birling: 'I accept no blame for it at all.'
Gerald: 'I'm rather more – upset…than I probably appear to be.'
Inspector: 'each of you helped to kill her. Remember that. Never forget it.'

AO3
Explain how Priestley's presentation of guilt links to his socialist message: characters **symbolise** their social class. The Birlings' refusal to accept guilt for Eva's death represents the upper class's exploitation of the working classes.

Through the lens of the upper-class Birling family, *An Inspector Calls* examines both individual and collective guilt, showing how societal prejudices, injustices and personal decisions interact[1]. As the Inspector reveals each character's involvement in the death of Eva/Daisy, the audience is invited to respond to their differing levels of guilt and their willingness to accept responsibility.

Priestley presents Mr Birling as a stereotypical uncaring capitalist of the early 20th century; the character who most clearly refuses to accept his guilt[2]. He describes his workers dismissively as 'labour costs' and tells Gerald and Eric that a man should 'look after himself' above others. He refuses to accept the Inspector's view that by sacking Eva/Daisy he started

[1] AO1: a sophisticated opening using key words from the question to show relevance.

[2] AO2/AO3: insight into how Priestley uses characterisation to explore political themes.

Paragraph	Content		Timing
1	Introduction – Priestley examines family life through the Birlings. He is mostly critical of them and the type of family relationships they represent.	Explain how Priestley's presentation of family life links to his criticism of social class.	9.35
2	Marriage – The Birling family connections prioritise appearance and social status over love. The house is 'substantial and heavily comfortable, but not cosy and homelike.'		9.45
	Husbands – Upper-class men (e.g. Arthur/Gerald) were expected to be the heads of families and prioritise wealth and social advancement.		

Essay plans and timings to help you plan more efficiently.

DO IT!

Now use what you've learned to answer the following AQA exam-style question.

How does Priestley explore ideas about power in *An Inspector Calls*?

Write about:

- the ideas about power in *An Inspector Calls*
- how Priestley presents these ideas by the way he writes.

[30 marks]

AQA exam-style questions using the *same* extract provided for the great answer analysis which precedes it.

Exam-style questions allow you to put into practice the skills you've learned and create a great answer by yourself.

Exam-style question 1

Online answers

Designed to guide you towards structuring a really 'great answer' and consolidate your understanding through thought and application (including an AO breakdown). Remember: it is important to write your own answers before checking online at **www.scholastic.co.uk/gcse**.

Advice for students

✓ **Know your text well.** This will help you to demonstrate your knowledge and understanding in the exam. Concentrate on knowing the text well rather than predicting questions.

✓ **Read the question carefully and answer the question.** Be sure you are answering the question you have chosen and *not* the one that you would have preferred to see on the paper.

✓ **Take time to think about and plan your answer.** Gathering your thoughts will give you space to address the question and choose appropriate references and details to support and develop your answer.

✓ **Demonstrate your knowledge by referencing parts of the novel.** But make sure it is relevant, you don't get extra marks for more **quotations**, but you do get more marks for making interesting comments about the references you have selected.

✓ **Read the extracts very carefully.** It is helpful to place the extract in the **context** of the novel – at what point, what happened before and/or after, which **characters** are involved, how does it link to other parts of the text. Be sure that you understand the meaning and context of quotations you choose from the extract.

✓ **Recognise that 'writer's methods' means anything the writer has done deliberately.** This covers the writer's use of language and techniques, the **structure** of the text and **characterisation**.

✓ **Understand the connection between the writer's methods and the writer's ideas.** It might be helpful to think about *how* the writer does something and *why* the writer does something.

✓ **Link comments on contextual factors/ideas to the text.** Keep in mind that context informs but should never dominate your reading of the text; the text comes first. Relating the extract to the whole text is a valid approach to context.

Question 1

How does Priestley explore ideas about guilt in *An Inspector Calls*?

Write about:

- the ideas about guilt in *An Inspector Calls*

- how Priestley presents these ideas by the way he writes.

[30 marks]

Zoom in on the question

How does Priestley explore ideas about guilt in *An Inspector Calls*

Write about:

- the ideas about guilt in *An Inspector Calls*
- how Priestley presents these ideas by the way he writes.

Consider what parts of the play relate to this theme and what Priestley wants the audience to think. (AO1)

Keep focused on the **language** and dramatic methods Priestley uses to influence the audience. (AO2)

Consider the play as a whole and how it relates to the time is was written and performed. (AO3)

Here are some ideas that could be included in an answer to this question which covers the Assessment Objectives (AOs):

AO1
Mr and Mrs Birling's refusal to accept their guilt. Sheila's guilt at having Eva fired/Eric's guilt at having abused her/Gerald's ambiguous response/the Inspector's role in uncovering the guilt of the Birlings.

AO2
Analysis of the differences between **characters** and how this is shown through their speech and action.

Mr Birling: 'a man has to…look after himself.'

Mrs Birling: 'I accept no blame for it at all.'

Gerald: 'I'm rather more – upset…than I probably appear to be.'

Inspector: 'each of you helped to kill her. Remember that. Never forget it.'

AO3
Explain how Priestley's presentation of guilt links to his socialist message: characters **symbolise** their social class. The Birlings' refusal to accept guilt for Eva's death represents the upper class's exploitation of the working classes.

A student has decided to focus on the responses of the Birling family to Eva/Daisy's death, rather than those of the Inspector. They argue that the difference in how the Birlings respond to their guilt is central to the play's political message about the upper classes.

This is the plan they have made to answer the question.

Paragraph	Content		Timing
1	Intro – main point: Priestley uses the Birlings as a lens to explore the nature of guilt, individual action and social responsibility.		9.35
2	Mr and Mrs Birling (older characters) are presented as self-interested. They are less developed, almost stereotypes of greed and snobbery. Mr Birling: 'a man…has to look after himself…' (Act One) Mrs Birling: 'I accept no blame for it at all.' (Act Two)	Start with how each character responds to the revelation of their role in Eva/Daisy's death. Consider what Priestley is saying *about* guilt – not just who is and isn't guilty.	9.45
3	Gerald is presented as more complex. He seems to feel guilty for his actions: consider his initial reaction to Daisy's death: 'My God!' (Act Two). He reverts to self-interest and tries to absolve the family from blame (Act Three).		9.55
4	Sheila and Eric are presented as more empathetic characters. Both accept their guilt and learn a moral lesson. Sheila: from 'so pleased with ourselves' (Act Two) to 'I still can't forget!' (Act Three). Eric: from 'a bit squiffy' (Act Three) to 'It frightens me too' (Act Three).		10.05
5	Conclusion: Ideas about guilt are important in understanding Priestley's condemnation of the upper classes. However, guilt can also lead to positive change.		10.15

The essay plan above will meet these Assessment Objectives:

AO1 Read, understand and respond	Considers the significance of the question focus (guilt) to the whole play. Uses relevant details to support arguments made, with a clear focus on the presentation of the Birling family and what they symbolise.
AO2 Language, form and structure	Focuses on Mr Birling's aggressive language and Mrs Birling's characterisation as cold. Gerald's development and how this contrasts with Eric's and Sheila's allows for analysis of structure, dialogue and characterisation.
AO3 Contexts	Explains how Priestley was concerned with exposing the immorality of the upper classes in 20th century Britain.

Notice...

As a way in to discussing the theme of guilt, the student structures their response around the presentation of individual characters. Each point analyses a character's 'guilt' in relation to their treatment of Eva/Daisy and then links to an overall discussion about Priestley's intentions as a playwright.

Through the lens of the upper-class Birling family, *An Inspector Calls* examines both individual and collective guilt, showing how societal prejudices, injustices and personal decisions interact[1]. As the Inspector reveals each character's involvement in the death of Eva/Daisy, the audience is invited to respond to their differing levels of guilt and their willingness to accept responsibility.

Priestley presents Mr Birling as a stereotypical uncaring capitalist of the early 20th century; the character who most clearly refuses to accept his guilt[2]. He describes his workers dismissively as 'labour costs' and tells Gerald and Eric that a man should 'look after himself' above others. He refuses to accept the Inspector's view that by sacking Eva/Daisy he started 'a chain of events' that led to her death. It is only after the Inspector has implicated all members of the family that he admits he would 'give thousands' of pounds to have acted differently. However, he appears motivated by fear of a public scandal, and is later quick to dismiss the Inspector's visit as 'hoaxing us'. In this way, Priestley suggests members of the upper classes such as Mr Birling feel no moral connection to those they perceive as socially inferior[3].

Similarly, Mrs Birling is presented as 'a rather cold woman' who refuses to understand how her decisions contribute to class exploitation. When a desperate Eva/Daisy seeks her assistance, Mrs Birling denies her money, despite knowing she is pregnant. The Inspector appeals to Mrs Birling's empathy as a mother, stating in forceful **declaratives**, 'You've had children. You must have known what she was feeling.' Mrs Birling excuses herself by hiding behind her role as charity organiser, stating, 'I accept no blame for it at all.' It is only once she realises that she might be personally affected – by the public revelation of Eric as the baby's father – that she becomes visibly 'distressed'[4]. By demonstrating pity for herself rather than guilt over Eva's death, Mrs Birling's presentation as uncaring mirrors that of her husband.

Gerald Croft initially seems to have a different response to guilt[5]. On hearing the news of Eva/Daisy's death, his broken syntax – 'My God!...I've suddenly realised...she's dead' – suggests a sincere sense of bereavement. He admits to having feelings for Daisy, and accepts

[1] AO1: a sophisticated opening using key words from the question to show relevance.

[2] AO2/AO3: insight into how Priestley uses characterisation to explore political themes.

[3] AO1: returns to question, making a perceptive point about the differing interpretations of guilt in the play.

[4] AO2: clear and perceptive analysis of dialogue.

[5] AO1: develops the argument by comparing the dramatic roles of different characters.

that his actions contributed to her death. In this way, Gerald seems to represent a more sympathetic image of the upper classes as being ignorant rather than cruel[6]. However, Gerald only accepts his guilt temporarily. When he returns at the end of Act Three, he appears more calculating, seeking to protect his reputation and questioning the authenticity of the Inspector's claims. Thus, Gerald embodies the internal conflict between moral responsibility and self-interest. Unlike Mr and Mrs Birling, who remain simplistic stereotypes, Gerald demonstrates a degree of emotional intelligence and character development. However, like the Birlings, he ultimately chooses to defend his reputation rather than feel remorse[7].

In contrast, Eric and Sheila's responses to their guilt are deep and immediate[8]. Sheila's reaction on being told how she affected Eva/Daisy displays the empathy her parents lack. She tells them: 'I still can't forget... It frightens me the way you talk.'[9] Eric, who admits he tipped Eva/Daisy to the point of suicide, agrees, stating 'It frightens me too'. Both younger characters have, by the play's end, understood how their individual actions contribute to broader social injustice.

In conclusion, through the lens of the Birling family, Priestley offers a powerful critique of the upper classes and their self-interest[10]. The play also explores the transformative nature of guilt, suggesting it can lead individuals to make positive changes. Sheila's final speech to her parents, in which she refers to 'the way you talk', suggests the younger generation have started to think for themselves and are choosing to reject the individualistic, capitalist ideology of their parents[11]. In this way, ideas about guilt are central to understanding Priestley's criticism of the ruling classes and his hope for a more compassionate future[12].

[6] **AO3**: awareness of the play's **context** and Priestley's political intentions.

[7] **AO2**: sophisticated analysis of characterisation.

[8] **AO1**: focus returns to the question.

[9] **AO2**: clear and detailed analysis of dialogue.

[10] **AO3**: links the concept of guilt to Priestley's political intentions as a playwright.

[11] **AO2**: an original and perceptive insight into a close detail.

[12] **AO1**: focus returns to the question.

Commentary

This is a very strong essay that starts with a clear response to the question. The argument is then developed with useful links between ideas. Supporting evidence considers characterisation at key moments, as well as character development and contrasts across the whole play. Appropriate terms are used throughout.

DO IT!

Now use what you've learned to answer the following AQA exam-style question.

How does Priestley explore ideas about power in *An Inspector Calls*?

Write about:

- the ideas about power in *An Inspector Calls*

- how Priestley presents these ideas by the way he writes.

[**30 marks**]

Question 2

How far can the Inspector be considered the hero of *An Inspector Calls*?

Write about:

- how J.B. Priestley writes about the Inspector
- in what ways the Inspector can be considered 'heroic'.

[30 marks]

Zoom in on the question

How far can the Inspector be considered the hero of *An Inspector Calls*?

Write about:
- how J.B. Priestley writes about the Inspector
- in what ways the Inspector can be considered 'heroic'.

Give your own personal view. You can agree or debate whether you believe the Inspector is the hero of the play. (AO1)

Keep focused on the language and dramatic methods Priestley uses to influence the audience. (AO2)

Consider what heroism means in general and why Priestley might want the audience to view characters in this way. (AO3)

Here are some ideas that could be included in an answer to this question which covers the Assessment Objectives (AOs):

AO1

The Inspector seeks justice for Eva/Daisy's death/refuses to be intimidated/is relentless in his pursuit of the truth. This suggests a divine/supernatural element to his character.
It could be argued that the Inspector is too judgemental to be heroic, and that he does not resolve anything by the end of the play.

AO2

Stage directions emphasise the Inspector's power and influence on arrival.
Dialogue during his interactions with Mr Birling emphasise his moral force.
The Inspector's final 'fire and blood and anguish' speech represents the play's main message about social justice.

AO3

Detectives – such as Sherlock Holmes and Hercule Poirot – were popular 'heroes' of literature at the time.
The Inspector can be seen as a mouthpiece for Priestley's socialist views. Does the character symbolise social justice and/or socialism?

A student has decided to argue that the Inspector can be seen as the hero. This is the plan for their answer.

Paragraph	Content		Timing
1	Main point – The view of the Inspector as heroic fits into the detective genre of the time. He uncovers a murder/seeks the truth.		9.40
2	Stage directions – The Inspector's arrival presents him as a character the Birlings can't ignore, when a 'sharp ring' of the doorbell interrupts Birling's speech about capitalism. He creates an 'impression of massiveness, solidity and purposefulness', emphasising his moral force.	Start with the question focus. Explain how each point influences the audience's reaction to the Inspector. At key points, explain why the Inspector can be seen as heroic and how this links to Priestley's political message.	9.45
3	The Inspector's speech dominates the play's dialogue and shapes the audience's view of events; his voice is described as 'cutting through, massively'. He is not intimidated by upper-class wealth and status. 'Public men, Mr Birling, have responsibilities as well as privileges.' (Act Two) He shows empathy for Eva/Daisy.		9.50
4	His actions drive the plot forward. He uncovers the truth/guilt of the Birlings and he stands for social justice. When he leaves, the Birlings stare 'subdued and wondering'.		9.55
5	Symbolic role – The Inspector appears as more than just a policeman enforcing the law; a divine/supernatural element to his character is hinted at.		10.05
6	Conclusion – The Inspector is heroic and acts as a mouthpiece for Priestley's socialist views.		10.15

The essay plan above will meet these Assessment Objectives:

AO1 Read, understand and respond	Considers the meaning of the question focus – whether the Inspector is heroic in the context of the play. Chooses relevant details to support arguments made, with a focus on how different elements of characterisation affect the audience's response.
AO2 Language, form and structure	Focuses on stage directions and specific language choices. Provides analysis of the play's structure, considering how the Inspector's presence and actions drive the plot: he questions the Birlings systematically to reveal the truth/seek justice.
AO3 Contexts	Considers how Priestley uses a popular genre – crime fiction – to make a broader political point.

Notice...
The student offers a clear argument to support the idea that the Inspector is a hero. In addition, the student undertakes a broader consideration of what the term 'hero' means in the context of the play's genre and the time the play was written.

As a character who plays a pivotal role in pursuing justice on behalf of poverty-stricken Eva Smith/Daisy Renton, the Inspector is clearly a heroic figure[1]. His character fits clearly into the style of 'whodunnit' detective fiction, popular at the time Priestley was writing in 1946[2]. This genre often centred around a resourceful detective who uncovered crime by piecing together evidence from a range of suspects. However, the Inspector's role is more complex, and the revelation that Inspector Goole may not be a real person implies an almost supernatural element to his character[3].

It can also be argued that the Inspector is symbolic of Priestley's own socialist viewpoint, and that he is investigating not just the Birling family but the social class they represent. This idea is immediately established in Act One when the Inspector's arrival is announced by 'the sharp ring of a front door bell', which interrupts Mr Birling's long-winded speech about the virtues of capitalism. On entering, the Inspector is described as creating an impression of 'massiveness, solidity and purposefulness' and speaking 'weightily'. This description emphasises his determination, the importance of his message and his moral force[4].

The Inspector refuses to be intimidated by wealth and power; when Mr Birling tries to assert his superiority, the Inspector states that 'Public men...have responsibilities as well as privileges'. He is described as 'cutting through, massively' to conversations and not allowing himself to be side-tracked from his duty[5]. He is also shown to care about Eva/Daisy and respect her as an individual[6], whereas the self-centred Birlings have treated her as an object. He describes her vulnerability as a young woman 'alone, friendless, almost penniless, desperate', yet – despite her challenges – able to look after herself. The Inspector's refusal to be intimidated and compassion establishes his heroic qualities[6].

Priestley's use of **dramatic tension** further emphasises the Inspector's role as hero. The revelation of Eva/Daisy's tragic story gradually unfolds with the Inspector meticulously building a case against each family member[7]. In the 'whodunnit' genre, this methodical approach showcases the Inspector's determination and thoroughness and creates a sense of anticipation as the audience begins to realise that each member of the Birling family is in some way responsible for Eva/Daisy's suicide. The Inspector comes to

[1] **AO1**: direct response to the question, using key terms.

[2] **AO3**: relevant link to literary context: how the Inspector would have been viewed by the audience at the time.

[3] **AO1**: opens up the question, establishing the basis for a more conceptual response.

[4] **AO2**: well-chosen details, focused analysis of language choices and accurate terminology.

[5] **AO2**: analysis of methods is systematic; moves from description to speech and action.

[6] **AO1**: effective summary point of previous paragraphs, linking back to the question.

represent the pursuit of truth on behalf of Eva/Daisy and the audience is naturally encouraged to be sympathetic towards him[6]. His final speech, which connects Eva/Daisy's suffering to broader social inequality – the 'millions and millions and millions of Eva Smiths and John Smiths' whose lives are 'intertwined with our lives' – is arguably the play's dramatic climax and the moment the Inspector appears the most heroic[7]. When he exits, leaving the Birlings standing 'subdued and wondering', there is a sense that justice has been served.

The revelation that 'there wasn't any Inspector Goole' on the police force develops the nature of this justice, suggesting that his authority is not just derived from a legal standpoint but one of conscience[8]. The revelation causes the characters to reflect on the Inspector's seeming omniscience: how, in Sheila's words, he 'never seemed like an ordinary police inspector' and 'we hardly ever told him anything he didn't know.'[9] This is supported by the stage directions that the lighting should become 'brighter and harder' when the Inspector enters, implying the revelation of sin. The Inspector's name – Goole – also implies a supernatural element (a ghoul, or ghost), and his final 'fire and blood and anguish' speech is almost Biblical in its language and warning to mankind to learn the lesson of collective responsibility or perish[9].

In conclusion, the Inspector's status as hero is clear, yet by the end of the play the audience realises that he is more than just a policeman 'doing my duty'. His language, and the impact he has on the Birling family and the audience, suggests that he is the embodiment of Priestley's own socialist views, representing the playwright's desire for a more egalitarian society[10].

[7] **AO2:** insight into how Priestley develops the portrayal of the Inspector through the play's structure. Apt summary of the **effect** on the audience, establishing the basis for a reading of the Inspector as political.

[8] **AO1:** the student makes careful use of synonyms for heroism (justice, conscience, moral force) to maintain focus on the question while developing own argument.

[9] **AO2:** further insightful analysis to support a more conceptual reading of the Inspector's character.

[10] **AO1/AO3:** the key concept of the essay is restated and connected to Priestley's political views.

Commentary

This is a well-structured and concise discussion of the question. The student starts with a clear conceptual argument, which they develop across the essay. They root their analysis in well-chosen details from the text, using quotes that are embedded seamlessly into the line of argument. The essay explores different dramatic techniques clearly, using appropriate terminology, and explains the intended effect on the audience of specific language choices.

DO IT!

Now use what you have learned to answer the following AQA exam-style question.

How far can Mrs Birling be considered the most unlikeable character in *An Inspector Calls*?

Write about:

- what Mrs Birling says and does throughout the play
- how far Mrs Birling can be considered unlikeable.

[30 marks]

Question 3

To what extent is Eric portrayed as an 'entirely selfish' character in *An Inspector Calls*?

Write about:

- what Eric says and does throughout the play

- the extent to which he can be considered 'entirely selfish'.

[30 marks]

Zoom in on the question

To what extent is Eric portrayed as an entirely selfish character in *An Inspector Calls*?

Write about:

- what Eric says and does throughout the play

- the extent to which he can be considered 'entirely selfish'.

Consider how Priestley wants the audience to react to Eric as a character. Consider how the question sets up areas for debate. (AO1)

Keep focused on the language and dramatic methods Priestley uses to characterise Eric. (AO2)

Consider the play as a whole and how it relates to the time is was written and performed. (AO3)

Here are some ideas that could be included in an answer to this question which covers the Assessment Objectives (AOs):

AO1	AO2	AO3
Eric only cares for himself – described as a 'drunken young idler' who steals money to protect himself. He also uses his wealthy position to prey on a vulnerable young woman. He is controlled by unloving parents. He challenges Mr Birling's view of the world. Ultimately, he takes responsibility for his actions.	Stage directions describe Eric as 'half shy, half assertive', hinting at two sides to his personality. He is described as having previously treated Eva/Daisy 'as if she was an animal'. He uses **euphemistic** phrases to play down his actions, saying 'that's when it happened' to describe raping Eva/Daisy. His character changes in Act Three; 'I did what I did' shows he accepts his guilt.	Consider how Eric fits into Priestley's political message and how a modern view might differ to that of a contemporary audience in 1946.

A student has decided to write an essay that focuses on the audience's changing reaction to Eric at different points in the play. This is the plan for their answer.

Paragraph	Content		Timing
1	Main point – Eric is presented as selfish at the start of the play, but is a complex character. By the end of the play, he demonstrates that he can accept responsibility for his actions.		9.35
2	Initial impression (Act One) – Description as 'half shy, half assertive' hints at two sides to his personality: selfish but unsure of himself and open to change.	Keep focused on the idea of selfishness. Explain how the audience's attitude to Eric changes as the play develops; don't just retell the story.	9.40
3	Treatment of Eva/Daisy (Act Two) – Tries to downplay his sexual assault of Eva/Daisy; describes it using euphemistic language common at the time: 'And that's when *it* happened.'		9.50
3	Inspector highlights Eric's selfishness: 'used her...as if she was an animal, a thing, not a person.'		9.50
4	Provides money for Eva/Daisy (Act Two) – 'I was in a state when I found out' – he doesn't abandon her when he finds out she is pregnant, but steals money from Mr Birling. Can be viewed as taking financial responsibility or as self-interest.		10.00
5	Accepts responsibility (Act Three) – 'I did what I did' (similar to what Sheila says); opposes his parents' view: 'You lot may be letting yourselves out nicely, but I can't.' Shows there are limits to Eric's selfishness and that he is open to change.		10.10
6	Conclusion – Eric behaves badly but is a more complex character than his parents. His willingness to accept responsibility reflects Priestley's hope for the younger generation.		10.15

The essay plan above will meet these Assessment Objectives:

AO1 Read, understand and respond	Considers the 'to what extent' element of the question focus. Eric is selfish, though he changes.
	Considers the different ways a character can be interpreted.
AO2 Language, form and structure	Analysis of structure: considers how Eric is presented at different points in the play through language choices.
	Analysis of form: considers how Eric compares to others in the play such as Sheila and his parents.
AO3 Contexts	Explores how Eric is used by Priestley to convey ideas about society and the future.
	Considers how a 21st century view of Eric's actions might differ.

Notice...

The student offers a debate in response to this question rather than choosing a one-sided line of argument. They unpick the subtleties of Eric's characterisation in how he developed across the whole play, addressing the nuances in specific language choices at key moments in the narrative.

In *An Inspector Calls*, Eric Birling is portrayed as a complex individual. While he behaves in a thoughtless and self-centred way for most of the play, by the end he demonstrates a willingness to accept responsibility and to change. It would therefore be inaccurate to say he is an entirely selfish character[1].

In Act One, Priestley implies there is more than one side to Eric's personality: he is described in the opening stage directions as 'in his early twenties, not quite at ease, half shy, half assertive.'[2] This simple pairing of **adjectives** (shy/assertive) suggests that Priestley wants the audience to believe that Eric still lacks confidence and is not quite fully formed as an individual, and therefore has the potential to change[3].

Nonetheless, it is undeniable that in many ways Eric's actions are selfish, reflecting the worst side of privileged upper-class male behaviour[4]. This is especially true when viewing the play from the perspective of the 21st century[5]. During the Inspector's questioning of Eric in Act Two, we learn how he abused Eva/Daisy several months after her affair with Gerald ended, when she was financially and emotionally at her lowest point. Eric also met her at the 'Palace Variety Theatre', implying that she has remained trapped in the same circumstances since her relationship with Gerald ended. Eva/Daisy is a 'bit' drunk when she meets Eric, 'chiefly because she'd not had much to eat that day', which connotes her continued poverty[6]. Priestley portrays Eric's behaviour as mirroring that of the predatory Alderman Meggarty; he takes advantage of Eva/Daisy's vulnerability by insisting on accompanying her home before, it is implied, drunkenly raping her[7]. Eric uses euphemistic language[8] here to downplay his behaviour, describing himself as being in 'that state when a chap easily turns nasty' and referring to rape as 'when it happened'. This euphemistic language was common in the early to mid-20th century and reflects the sexist and misogynistic stereotypes that Eric draws on to justify his treatment of Eva/Daisy[9]. He continues to see her and have sex with her, although he 'wasn't in love with her or anything' – she just proved to be a 'good sport'. In this, Eric is directly challenged by the Inspector, who tells him that he has used her 'as if she was an animal, a thing, not a person'. This intentional use of **dysphemism** places Eric's behaviour into a new light: Priestley is making

1 AO1: starts with a clear conceptual idea of Eric's role in the play. Sets up both sides of the argument.

2 AO2: clear, close analysis of language choices with well-selected supporting detail.

3 AO2: uses subject terminology effectively. Clear analysis of **effect** of language choices.

4 AO1: returns to the question, offering a clear line of argument.

5 AO3: shows understanding of the play's context.

6 AO2: neatly summarises action of the play that supports this reading of the play

7 AO2: develops the point through close analysis of text and comparison to other characters.

8 AO2: uses sophisticated subject terminology.

9 AO3: makes specific links between the play and the values of the time.

it clear to the audience how he has used his powerful position to selfishly exploit a vulnerable working-class girl[10].

It can be argued that Eric's actions after this point demonstrate a level of concern for Eva/Daisy[11], suggesting there is a limit to his selfishness. On learning that she is pregnant, rather than abandoning her, he describes himself as being in 'a hell of a state about it'. It is implied that he discusses marriage with Eva, showing some consideration of her reputation, and tries to support her financially by stealing money from his father. However, Eric's reaction can also be seen as a panicked attempt to avoid the consequences of his actions. The 'state' he was in is ambiguous; was it a genuine realisation of what he had done, or concern for his own position?[12]

On the other hand, by the end of the play, Eric has clearly learned a lesson, accepting responsibility for his role in Eva/Daisy's suicide when he states 'the fact remains that I did what I did' and refusing to let himself 'out nicely' like Gerald and his parents do[13].

In conclusion, while Eric is self-centred and treats Eva/ Daisy badly, he is a complex rather than a cartoonish character who has the potential for reform[13]. In this, Eric can be seen to represent Priestley's faith in a younger generation who may learn to avoid the mistakes of their parents' generation.

[10] **AO2/AO3**: makes concise link between Priestley's use of dramatic devices and his political message.

[11] **AO1**: returns to question focus but from a slightly different angle and offers a counter view.

[12] **AO2**: makes a perceptive point, evaluating the same detail from different perspectives, with concise use of supporting detail.

[13] **AO1**: clear engagement with the 'to what extent' part of the question.

Commentary

This essay demonstrates a perceptive view of Eric's characterisation and establishes a clear discussion about the extent to which he can be considered selfish. Concise, well-chosen quotations along with summaries of action and the play's structure are used effectively to support the student's analysis. All references to the play's context are relevant to the point being made.

DOIT!

Now use what you've learned to answer the following AQA exam-style question.

To what extent is Sheila portrayed as a decent and caring character?

Write about

- what Sheila says and does throughout the play

- the extent to which she can be considered 'decent' and 'caring'.

[30 marks]

Question 4

How far does Priestley criticise the values and behaviour of the upper classes in *An Inspector Calls*?

Write about

- how Priestley presents the upper classes through the way he writes

- the extent to which the play can be a read as a criticism of the values and behaviours of the upper classes.

[30 marks]

Zoom in on the question

How far does Priestley criticise the values and behaviour of the upper classes in *An Inspector Calls*?

Write about

- how Priestley presents the upper classes through the way he writes

- the extent to which the play can be a read as a criticism of the values and behaviours of the upper classes.

Consider which elements of the play relate to this theme. Consider how the audience should react. (AO1)

Explain how this reaction is created through Priestley's choices as a playwright. (AO2)

Consider the play as a whole and how it relates to the time is was written and performed. (AO3)

Here are some ideas that could be included in an answer to this question which covers the Assessment Objectives (AOs):

AO1
Explore Priestley's presentation of the Birlings as representative of the upper classes, and Eva/Daisy as representative of the working classes.
Consider how Eva/Daisy's death symbolises the human cost of exploitative upper-class values and behaviours.

AO2
Consider Priestley's presentation of the Birlings as cold and selfish, and Eva/Daisy's presentation as a victim, and how the audience is expected to react to them. Mr Birling unfairly sacks Eva for requesting better pay; Sheila has her fired out of jealousy; Gerald and Eric exploit her sexually; Sybil refuses her charity because of prejudice.

AO3
Explain how Priestley's presentation of the Birlings links to the play's political message: the Birling family represents a capitalistic view of society; they are portrayed as selfish and ignorant.

A student has decided to write an essay that focuses on the audience's first impressions of the Birling family, and their differing responses to Eva/Daisy's death. This is the plan for their answer.

Paragraph	Content		Timing
1	Introduction – Priestley was a socialist. The Birlings represent the upper classes and the play is a criticism of their values and behaviour.		9.40
2	First impressions – The Birlings are introduced as materialistic, prioritising wealth and appearance over people: their home is described as 'substantial and heavily comfortable but not cosy and homelike'.	Refer back to question focus. Consider the play's context. Remember that characters in the play symbolise different political viewpoints.	9.45
3 & 4	Values of the upper classes – Mr Birling celebrates capitalism and rejects 'community and all that nonsense', 'all mixed up together like bees in a hive...a man has to mind his own business and look after himself.' Gerald supports Birling's view that there is a need to 'come down sharply on some of these people.' Eva's suicide ('died, after several hours of agony') shows the human consequences of the upper classes lack of compassion.		9.55
5	Behaviours of the upper classes – Eva/Daisy's story shows how each member of the family contributed to her death through their behaviour. Summarise here the 'chain of events' that connects each character to Eva/Daisy's death.		10.05
6	Conclusion – Although some characters are remorseful, the play as a whole is a political criticism of the upper classes.		10.15

The essay plan above will meet these Assessment Objectives:

AO1 Read, understand and respond	Gives a clear interpretation of the question. Offers an argument for how Priestley shapes the audience's response to the upper classes. Makes a clear and relevant distinction between values and behaviours.
AO2 Language, form and structure	Language and structure: supports analysis of opening stage directions and how these frame the audience response. Characterisation and structure: supports analysis of language in the speech of Birling and the Inspector. Demonstrates how characters represent different ideas.
AO3 Contexts	Clearly focuses on the political message of the play, considering the time in which it was written and performed.

Notice…

The student starts with a clear sense of historical context and outlines Priestley's intentions as a playwright. They move on to analyse Mr Birling's speech in close detail, demonstrating how it exemplifies the social values that Priestley seeks to attack, before showing how the characters' behaviours across the play demonstrate the negative consequences of such beliefs.

Priestley was a socialist who believed in equality and holding those with wealth and power to account. It can be argued that Priestley set the play in 1912 as a way of criticising the values and behaviour of the previous generation's ruling class who, in his view, had exploited the working classes and led Britain into twenty years of social division and war ❶.

❶ AO1/AO3: a concise introduction that recognises the question is about the political intentions of the play.

Taken as a whole, *An Inspector Calls* can be seen as a polemical attack on the values and behaviour of the wealthy Birling family and the aristocratic Gerald Croft ❷. The stage directions in Act One implicitly criticise the family, presenting them as cold and self-centred, suggesting they prioritise wealth and appearance over caring for others. The dining room is 'substantial and heavily comfortable but not cosy and homelike', and although the Birlings appear like a 'nice well-behaved family', even before the Inspector's arrival there are suggestions of hidden secrets ❸. For example, we are told that Gerald 'never came near' Sheila the previous summer, **foreshadowing** his deceit and sexual betrayal; Eric is clearly hiding a drinking problem; and Mr Birling seems to care about his daughter's engagement only in as far as it serves his business interests.

❷ AO1: a clear and unambiguous line of argument that shows a sophisticated understanding of Priestley's politics.

❸ AO2: close analysis of how the play's stage directions and dialogue combine to create meaning.

Describing himself as a 'hard-headed, practical man of business', Mr Birling gives a lengthy speech about his view of society, rejecting the idea of community. He tells Eric and Gerald that 'a man has to make his own way', and the idea that we are 'all mixed up together like bees in a hive' is 'nonsense' ❹. The audience therefore associates Birling with capitalist individualism. Priestley then cleverly undermines Birling's position ❺ using **dramatic irony:** ❻ Mr Birling confidently dismisses 'wild talk' about 'possible labour trouble' and fears of war as 'nonsense' from 'a few scaremongers'. To an audience who had lived through the Great Depression and two world wars, this establishes Mr Birling as a foolish character whose viewpoint is not to be trusted. This is reinforced by Mr Birling's belief that the newly built *Titanic* is 'absolutely unsinkable' ❼.

❹ AO2: discussion of Mr Birling's speech supported effectively with a range of examples.

❺ AO1: clearly explains the intended effect on the audience, showing how Priestley shapes the audience's response to the upper classes.

❻ AO2: considers the text in performance using appropriate terminology ('dramatic irony').

❼ AO3: demonstrates a clear understanding of the context in which the play was written and performed.

Priestley uses the story of Eva/Daisy to criticise upper-class behaviour. Dialogue between Birling and Gerald shows how capitalists collaborated to keep employees' wages down[8]. Explaining why he refused the requested pay rise, Mr Birling says employers need to 'come down sharply on some of these people' or 'they'd soon be asking for the earth.' The Inspector's graphic description of Eva/Daisy's death provides a stark contrast to this view: as a pregnant, unmarried, jobless woman Eva/Daisy was so desperate that she killed herself by drinking disinfectant[9]. Thus, the consequences of upper-class contempt for the working classes are clearly shown[10].

Through the play, we learn how each of the Birlings have in some way contributed to Eva/Daisy's death. Sheila had her sacked from Milwards department store; Gerald used his wealth and status to 'install' her in his friend's flat and have an affair with her; Eric took Eva/Daisy home when she was at her weakest and drunkenly raped her; Mrs Birling refused to provide her with financial support from the charity organisation she runs[11]. However, it can be argued that Priestley is less critical of some upper-class characters than others. For example, Gerald does seem to have had some genuine affection for Eva/Daisy, and by the end of the play Eric and Sheila feel genuine remorse for their poor treatment of her[12].

As a **polemicist**, however[13], Priestley was mostly interested in broader social themes. Although somewhat concerned with individual behaviour, the Inspector's **metaphor** of society as 'one body' is key to understanding the play's real message[13]: while *An Inspector Calls* is a play about one family and one victim, Priestley's anger at the sense of entitlement and selfishness of the upper classes in general shines through – from start to finish[14].

[8] **AO1**: develops argument, balancing discussion of the whole play with specific examples.

[9] **AO2**: analysis is clear and fluent, using simple but effective subject terminology (description/contrast)

[10] **AO1**: summarises point by returning to the question.

[11] **AO2**: summary of the plot and action supports the overall argument with relevant details and language from the question embedded.

[12] **AO1**: addresses the 'to what extent' element of the question.

[13] **AO1**: 'However' clearly signals the student's conclusion.

[14] **AO1/AO3**: returns to the main issue of the question, and ends with a definitive interpretation of the political message of the play.

Commentary
This is an insightful analysis of Priestley's political intentions as a playwright, clearly argued and rooted in the play's context. The student distinguishes between the play as a piece of drama and a polemic. Examples are concisely integrated into the analysis, using an subject-specific terminology. The student clearly links the text to the presentation of political values, with insightful points about structure and audience.

DO IT!

Now use what you've learned to answer the following AQA exam-style question.

How far does Priestley criticise the behaviour of male characters towards women in *An Inspector Calls*?

Write about:
- how Priestley presents male characters in *An Inspector Calls* through the way he writes
- the extent to which the play can be read as a criticism of male behaviour towards women.

[30 marks]

Question 5

How does Priestley use Eva Smith/Daisy Renton to explore ideas about exploitation and inequality in *An Inspector Calls*?

Write about:

- how Priestley presents Eva Smith/Daisy Renton through the play

- how Eva Smith/Daisy Renton is used as a character to explore ideas about exploitation and inequality.

[30 marks]

Zoom in on the question

How does Priestley use Eva Smith/Daisy Renton to explore ideas about exploitation and inequality in *An Inspector Calls*?

Write about:

- how Priestley presents Eva Smith/Daisy Renton through the play

- how Eva Smith/Daisy Renton is used as a character to explore ideas about exploitation and inequality.

Choose your own ideas for this question. What types of power and inequality does the play explore? How does Eva/Daisy link to this theme? (AO1)

Consider how Eva/Daisy is described, what happens to her and how the audience is expected to respond. (AO2)

Keep focused on Priestley's intentions as a political playwright and the social issues at the time the play was written and performed. (AO3)

Here are some ideas that could be included in an answer to this question which covers the Assessment Objectives (AOs):

AO1
Eva/Daisy represents the exploitation of the working classes. She has no power over her life.
Eva/Daisy is systematically mistreated by her employers and abused by powerful men. She symbolises the double inequality faced by working-class women in Edwardian society.

AO2
Consider how Eva/Daisy is described by others.
The more powerful characters objectify her: Mr Birling sees her as 'labour costs'; Eric sees her as 'pretty and a good sport'.
Consider how this contrasts with the Inspector's belief that there are 'millions and millions and millions of Eva Smiths' in every society, and that 'We are responsible for each other.'

AO3
Consider how the presentation of Eva/Daisy fits with Priestley's criticism of class and gender within Edwardian society. Eva/Daisy represents 'millions and millions and millions' of working-class women who were vulnerable to exploitation and didn't have a political voice.

A student has chosen to write an essay that focuses on Eva/Daisy as a symbol for the inequality faced by working-class women at the time the play was set. This is the plan they have made to answer the question.

Paragraph	Content		Timing
1	Introduction – The treatment of Eva/Daisy represents the exploitation of working-class people in the early 20th century. Her death provides the moral centre of the play.		9.40
2	The significance of her name – Eva/Daisy suggests vulnerability and anonymity; she is an ordinary person. The Inspector says there are 'millions and millions and millions of Eva Smiths'; his speech reminds the audience that she represents a whole social group.	Refer back to the question at the end of each paragraph.	9.50
3	Living conditions/death – Eva/Daisy is described as stuck in poverty – 'counting... pennies' in a 'dingy little back bedroom'. This provides a stark contrast with the wealth and luxury of the Birlings' 'prosperous' house.	Comment on the significance of key vocabulary choices and explain how and why Priestley wanted the audience of 1946 to respond.	9.55
4	Systemic class oppression – Eva/Daisy is caught in a downward spiral that pushes her to suicide: a 'chain of events' in which each aspect of her life is defined or controlled by more powerful characters.		10.05
5	Double inequality – Eva/Daisy is working class but also female, which makes her vulnerable to sexual exploitation and hypocrisy (Gerald/Eric).		10.10
6	Conclusion – Eva/Daisy's fate is central to Priestley's message. She is defined by others – and doesn't appear on stage.		10.15

The essay plan above will meet these Assessment Objectives:

AO1 Read, understand and respond	Provides a conceptual response to the question. Sets up a structured argument for how Priestley uses the character of Eva/Daisy to shape the audience's reaction and comment on power and inequality in society.
AO2 Language, form and structure	Explores characterisation from a range of perspectives: names used to refer to characters; setting and language; action and contrast. Considers structure of play: how information about Eva's life and symbolic role is revealed.
AO3 Contexts	Clearly focuses on Priestley's political ideas. Provides discussion of beliefs and values of the time towards poverty, social responsibility and gender.

Notice...

This student writes with confidence throughout. Each paragraph is based around a different element of Eva/Daisy's characterisation, with precise details drawn from across the play to support the development of the overall argument.

The character of Eva Smith/Daisy Renton is Priestley's symbol for the exploitation of working-class people in the early 20th century[1]. She is subject to mistreatment at the hands of individuals with power, being fired from her job and abused sexually by wealthy men. The treatment of Eva/Daisy highlights the power dynamics at play in Edwardian England, and her violent suicide can be considered the moral centre of *An Inspector Calls*[2].

Priestley chose Eva/Daisy's names to represent the anonymity of working-class people. As the Inspector tells the Birlings at the end of Act Three, there are 'millions and millions and millions of Eva Smiths' in society. Having more than one name further emphasises her universality and suggests that, to those in power, Eva/Daisy is 'a thing, not a person'[3].

Eva/Daisy's vulnerability is emphasised throughout the play. Whereas the Birlings live in wealth and luxury, Eva's poverty is repeatedly highlighted. We are told of her hunger and given images of her 'counting...pennies'[3] in a 'dingy little back bedroom'[3]. After unfairly losing two jobs and her reputation, it is twice implied that she may have been forced into prostitution[3] before eventually killing herself in desperation[3]. At the time the play was written, there was no welfare state and very little support for unemployed people. One of Priestley's main reasons for writing the play was to expose the injustice of this inequality[4].

Another idea that Eva/Daisy's character represents is the systemic nature of class oppression[5]. Each character contributes to her downward spiral in what the Inspector calls 'a chain of events'. Mr Birling fires her for demanding better working conditions; Sheila has her fired for looking 'impertinent'; and Mrs Birling rejects her plea for financial assistance when she is destitute. Although no individual member of the Birling family kills Eva/Daisy, as a social class they are collectively responsible for her death[6].

Another way to view Eva/Daisy's character is as representative of the double inequality faced by working-class females at the time the play was set. In 1912, women could not vote or own property; perceptions of women at the time would most likely be considered deeply misogynistic today[7]. Throughout the play, male characters objectify women in their choice of

---

[1] AO1: a concise beginning that offers a conceptual argument.

[2] AO3: makes links to social context and Priestley's political ideas.

[3] AO2: offers an effective analysis of how ideas are presented at different points in the play.

[4] AO3: successfully links to Priestley's views and play's context.

[5] AO1: develops question focus.

[6] AO1: develops conceptual argument.

[7] AO3: places argument effectively in historical context.

language. Eva/Daisy is described by Gerald as 'fresh and charming' in comparison to the other 'hard-eyed dough-faced women' at the Palace Variety Theatre, and Eric describes her as 'good sport'. Gerald becomes her 'wonderful Fairy Prince' only to abandon her when their relationship becomes inconvenient; later, she is sexually abused by Alderman Meggarty and raped by Eric[8]. When Eva/Daisy realises she is pregnant as a result of this abuse, Mrs Birling cruelly blames her for her predicament, dismissing her as 'a girl of that sort'. These descriptions of Eva/Daisy as a vulnerable victim contrast powerfully with the Inspector's initial shocking image of Daisy in Act One as a suicide victim who has 'Burnt her inside out' with disinfectant[9].

[8] **AO2**: range of details drawn together to effectively analyse characterisation.

[9] **AO2**: a perceptive link that draws together seemingly unconnected details from across the play, showing how they develop the theme.

In conclusion, Priestley uses the character of Eva/Daisy to demonstrate the powerlessness of working-class women and the devastating consequences of gender and class inequality. Her tragic suicide is a **catalyst** for the Inspector's search for social and personal justice and serves as a warning for the audience, encouraging them to reconsider the impact of their actions on other people and society as a whole. Perhaps the most significant aspect of the presentation of Eva/Daisy is the fact that she herself is not present in the play – it is an irony that while the Inspector seeks to give Eva/Daisy a voice and achieve justice on her behalf, her life story is told by other, more powerful people[10].

[10] **AO1**: effective summary of argument which makes dramatic and thematic links.

Commentary

This short answer is based on a clear, conceptual idea about the symbolic role of Eva/Daisy. The points are structured around the ideas that she represents, which means the student avoids simply retelling her story. Instead, precise examples are drawn from different points in the narrative, demonstrating excellent knowledge of the plot. The student's argument is rooted in a solid understanding of the play's context and develops in interesting ways to produce a highly perceptive analysis of characterisation.

DO IT!

Now use what you've learned to answer the following AQA exam-style question.

How does Priestley use Eva Smith/Daisy Renton to explore ideas about the effect of poverty in *An Inspector Calls*?

Write about:

- how Priestley presents Eva Smith/Daisy Renton through the way he writes
- how Priestley uses the character of Eva Smith/Daisy Renton to explore the effects of poverty.

[30 marks]

'All relationships in *An Inspector Calls* are based on deception.'

How far do you agree with this description of the play?

Write about:

- how different characters and events in the play explore this idea

- what Priestley wants the audience to think about different types of relationships.

[30 marks]

Zoom in on the question

'All relationships in *An Inspector Calls* are based on deception.'

How far do you agree with this description of the play?

Write about:
- how different characters and events in the play explore this idea

- what Priestley wants the audience to think about different types of relationships.

> Notice the question invites debate. Consider if this is true of all relationships at all points in the play. (AO1)

> Discuss a range of examples from across the play. Focus on how Priestley writes about them. (AO2)

> Consider how Priestley's presentation of the theme links to his political views and the time the play was written/performed. (AO3)

Here are some ideas that could be included in an answer to this question which covers the Assessment Objectives (AOs):

AO1

Deception in romantic relationships: Gerald and Sheila.
Deception in family relationships: Eric/Sheila/Mrs Birling.
The Inspector as an antidote to deception.
Gerald's view of himself – a kind of self-deception?
Mr Birling's attempts to deceive the Inspector.
The Inspector's deception of the Birling family by acting as a real policeman.

AO2

How hidden tensions are implied and then revealed through dialogue.
Sheila to Gerald: 'last summer, when you never came near me.'
Gerald to Birling: 'You seem to be a nice well-behaved family.'
How characters display honesty to each other at key points.
How the play as a whole moves from deception to revelation of the truth.

AO3

Priestley's presentation of the upper classes as deceitful is part of the play's political argument.
The influence of strict social attitudes towards relationships, and how Edwardian society encouraged emotional repression.

A student has decided to write an essay focusing on deception in the relationships between Eric and his family and between Gerald and Sheila. This is the plan they have made to answer the question.

Paragraph	Content		Timing
1	Introduction – Most relationships contain deception; link to Priestley's attack on upper classes. The Inspector unravels layers of deceit to expose the truth.		9.40
2	Parent/child relationships – Eric and Sheila are distant from their strict parents and hide their feelings/behaviour. Birling sees Gerald's marriage to Sheila as a business opportunity: 'your engagement to Sheila means a tremendous lot to me...Crofts and Birlings are no longer competing but are working together – for lower costs and higher prices.' Eric hides his drinking and unhappiness: Mrs Birling says to him, 'you're not that type – you don't get drunk.'	Avoid retelling the story and simply agreeing with the statement. Consider different types of relationship in the play and look for areas of debate in the question.	9.50
3	Romantic relationships/marriage – Mr and Mrs Birling's relationship appears to be based on money and superficial appearances. Gerald hides his affair with Eva/Daisy from Sheila: 'all last summer...you never came near me.' Gerald is guilty of self-deception: Sheila describes him as playing the role of, 'the wonderful Fairy Prince'.		10.00
4	Counter-arguments – Sheila to Gerald: 'I rather respect you more than I've ever done before.' Eric to Mr Birling: 'you're not the kind of father a chap could go to when he's in trouble.' Sheila to her family by the play's end: (passionately) 'You're pretending everything's just as it was before.' Deception is revealed at key points and the characters begin to speak honestly to each other.		10.10
5	Conclusion – The rejection of hypocrisy and deception by the play's younger characters (Sheila, Eric) reflects Priestley's hope for the younger generation.		10.15

The essay plan above will meet these Assessment Objectives:

AO1 Read, understand and respond	Offers a range of ideas from across the text. Clearly engages with counter arguments.
AO2 Language, form and structure	Explores what characters say and do. Considers differences in presentation of different relationships.
AO3 Contexts	Understands how ideas about relationship from the time are presented. Explores how Priestley uses the theme of deceit to present his political views.

Notice...
The student starts by addressing the theme of deceit in the play as a whole, considering how it links to Priestley's intentions as a political writer. They then deal with the different relationships between characters in separate but linked paragraphs.

The theme of deception runs throughout *An Inspector Calls*: most relationships involve some level of deceit. The Birlings lie, steal and betray each other while maintaining the outward façade of a 'nice well-behaved family'❶. Through his unwavering questions, the Inspector unravels the Birlings' lies, and in this way, J.B. Priestley exposes upper-class hypocrisy❷. Yet the play offers a more nuanced portrayal of romantic and family relationships than the above statement might suggest❸.

Both Eric and Sheila's relationships with their parents❹ are marred by a lack of emotional connection, leading to hidden tensions and deceit❹. Exemplifying Edwardian upper-class views on parenting, Mr and Mrs Birling appear more concerned with their social status than their children's welfare❷. This is shown in the way Mr Birling describes his daughter's engagement to Gerald Croft as a business opportunity – a chance for 'Crofts and Birlings' to work 'together for lower costs and higher prices' – rather than a relationship based on love and respect. Similarly, from the start it is implied that Eric has an alcohol addiction and is leading a double life – despite Mrs Birling's insistence that Eric is 'not the type' to 'get drunk'. A key revelation here is that Eric raped Eva while intoxicated, left her pregnant and stole money to support her. When asked why he lied, Eric replies angrily to Mr Birling 'you're not the kind of father a chap could go to when he's in trouble', suggesting that Eric has always felt the need to lie to maintain their relationship❺. It can be argued that Priestley's intention here is to criticise the strict patriarchal values that Mr Birling represents❻.

The play's main romantic relationships❼ are also shown to be based on lies and pretence. Mr and Mrs Birling's relationship seems defined by money, and while Gerald and Sheila's engagement initially seems harmonious, there are hints from the start that Gerald has been unfaithful. In an opening exchange, Sheila – *'half serious, half playful'* – mentions that Gerald avoided her the previous summer; it is later revealed that during this time he had been conducting an affair with Eva/ Daisy, whom he met at the Palace Variety Theatre, a 'favourite haunt of women of the town' (a **euphemism** for prostitutes). Gerald gave her money and accommodation, becoming 'the most important person in her life', before abandoning her for his more socially advantageous engagement.

❶ **AO1:** perceptive opening that provides a concise focus on the question.

❷ **AO3:** relevant link to context.

❸ **AO2:** consideration of how and why Priestley achieves this effect.

❹ **AO1:** expands focus on the question: different types of relationships.

❺ **AO2:** perceptive analysis that summarises structure and character and uses well-selected details to evidence their reading.

❻ **AO3:** considers Priestley's intent.

❼ **AO1:** further develops focus of essay, commenting on different types of relationships.

The revelation of his affair shatters the illusion of his commitment to Sheila and leads to the breakdown of their relationship[8]. Gerald is shown to be guilty of deceiving both women and, as Sheila intimates, he is also guilty of self-deception, seeing himself as 'the wonderful Fairy Prince' while actually using his wealth and power to manipulate Eva/Daisy for sex.

However, this view of Gerald reduces him to a stereotype and misses some of the complexities of his character. Some productions of the play imply that Gerald genuinely cared for Eva/Daisy and can speak honestly with Sheila[9]. There is certainly evidence for this. On hearing of Eva/Daisy's death, the stage direction describes Gerald as 'startled' and 'distressed', exclaiming 'My God!... I've suddenly realised – taken it in properly – that she's dead – '. He admits that his feelings towards Eva were ambiguous, and after returning her engagement ring, Sheila tells him she respects him for his honesty.

In conclusion, it can be argued that all relationships within the play contain an element of deceit, which is gradually revealed and resolved. For example, though Eric and Sheila's relationships with their parents were initially characterised by deceit and tension, by the end of the play Eric speaks more directly to his father, suggesting the emotional maturity to think for himself, and Sheila insists that her parents are wrong in 'pretending everything's just as it was before'. These signal to the audience that the younger members of the family have rejected the deception and hypocrisy of their parents' generation[10]. The importance of taking responsibility for the consequences of deceitful behaviour is therefore a key message of the play.

[8] **AO2**: shows clear understanding of characterisation, supported with relevant details. Perceptive reading of Priestley's language choices.

[9] **AO1/AO3**: clear engagement with 'to what extent'. Argument supported by context of play's performance/interpretation.

[10] **AO1**: implicitly links back to question and Priestley's intent.

Commentary
This a well-focused essay that effectively engages with the debate in a subtle way. Throughout the essay the student carefully considers the way 'deception' operates in different types of relationships and at different points in the narrative. They successfully analyse and explain why Priestley presents relationships in the play for dramatic and thematic purposes, while also considering how various performers and readers of the play might differ in their interpretations. Context is used effectively, and the range of terminology is appropriate.

DO IT!

Now use what you've learned to answer the following AQA exam-style question.

'The characters in *An Inspector Calls* only seem to care about themselves.'

How far do you agree with this description of the play?

Write about:

- how different relationships and events in the play explore this idea

- what Priestley wants the audience to think about different characters and why.

[30 marks]

Question 7

How does Priestley use the setting and **stagecraft** of *An Inspector Calls* to convey his ideas?

Write about:

- how Priestley uses the locations and set of the play to convey different ideas

- how Priestley uses lighting, **props** or stage directions to affect the audience's response.

[30 marks]

Zoom in on the question

How does Priestley use the setting and stagecraft of *An Inspector Calls* to convey his ideas?

Write about:

- how Priestley uses the locations and set of the play to convey different ideas

- how Priestley uses lighting, props or stage directions to affect the audience's response.

Notice how this question focuses on the dramatic/ literary techniques rather than a specific theme. (AO1)

The bullet points give you further information about what 'setting and stage craft' means. (AO2)

Consider the play as a whole and what Priestley wanted to say about society. (AO3)

Here are some ideas that could be included in an answer to this question which covers the Assessment Objectives (AOs):

AO1	AO2	AO3
Setting: the whole play takes place in the Birlings' dining room. Lighting is used to indicate changes in mood and **atmosphere**. Stage directions guide the actors' movements and interactions. Props: photos of Eva/the telephone/ the doorbell are used for dramatic effect at key moments of the play.	How setting is used to shape the audience's response to the Birling family and the values they represent. How Priestley uses stage directions to convey changes in **characters'** emotions and relationships, and how this affects the audience's response. How props and setting are used to help build tension and create a sense of confinement.	Consider how the play functions in the context of performance. Consider how Priestley uses setting and stagecraft to convey his criticism of British society.

A student has decided to write an essay that argues setting and stagecraft help Priestley convey ideas about social class and tensions between the Birlings and the Inspector. This is the plan they have made to answer the question.

Paragraph	Content		Timing
1	Introduction – The play's setting and stagecraft shapes the audience's view of the Birling family, creates dramatic tension, and conveys ideas about inequality.		9.35
2	Setting – Birlings' dining room, described in the stage directions as *substantial and heavily comfortable* with *'champagne glasses'*, represents upper-class privilege and contrasts with Eva's poverty.	Refer back to the question at the end of each paragraph.	9.40
3	Lighting – *'The lighting should be pink and intimate until the INSPECTOR arrives, and then it should be brighter and harder.'* Changes in lighting on the Inspector's arrival symbolise that he will interrogate the Birlings, and this process will be uncomfortable for them.	Remember to include quotes from stage directions.	9.45
4	Props – The photo of Eva/Daisy symbolises her absence and forces the Birlings to confront their responsibility for her. It connects the Birlings and the audience to the character of Eva/Daisy.	Descriptions of staging and line delivery count as language analysis.	9.50
5	Stage directions – These are used to illustrate the differences and tensions between the Birling family and the Inspector. BIRLING (*rather impatiently*) SHEILA (*rather distressed*) GERALD (*hesitatingly*) MRS B. (*with dignity*)		10.00
6	Conclusion – Priestley uses stagecraft for powerful dramatic and symbolic impact in *An Inspector Calls.*		10.15

The essay plan above will meet these Assessment Objectives:

AO1 Read, understand and respond	Considers a broad range of elements from the question.
	Focuses on the role of setting and stagecraft in both driving the narrative and conveying Priestley's ideas about inequality and social class.
AO2 Language, form and structure	Considers elements of performance and structure as well as language and character.
AO3 Contexts	The response is based on a clear understanding of Priestley's political views and dramatic form.

Notice...
The student considers the play as a piece of theatre, not just a written text. They start by explaining Priestley's intentions as a dramatist and then structure each point around a different element of setting or stagecraft. Each point links back to the intended dramatic impact and how it helps convey specific ideas.

An *Inspector Calls* is set in 1912 in a fictional industrial city called Brumley, 'in the North Midlands', and all action occurs over the course of a single evening in one location – the dining room of the Birling family home. Mr Birling himself is described as a 'prosperous manufacturer'[1]. Thus, Priestley draws on the **three unities** idea of dramatic impact, focusing on a single event that plays out in real time, in a single location. As a result, the audience's emotional response is heightened as the Inspector gradually exposes the Birlings' collective guilt in front of them.

[1] AO1: introduction offers a clear overview of the areas the essay will discuss and introduces the argument it will develop.

The opening description of the Birling family's dining room is one of luxury, signifying their upper-class lifestyle. The furniture is 'substantial and heavily comfortable'; the table covered with 'dessert plates and champagne glasses'; Edna, 'the parlour-maid', is '*replacing them with decanter of port, cigar box and cigarettes*'. All five family members are wearing formal 'evening dress'. The focus on the opulence of their lifestyle suggests how isolated and cushioned they are from the poverty and suffering of others[2]. The Birlings represent the wealthy business owners who had become increasingly powerful in the late 19th and early 20th centuries following the industrial revolution. As a socialist writer, Priestley seeks to criticise this social class throughout the play[3]. After the Inspector's arrival, this contrast becomes starker through descriptions of the poverty and 'dingy' living conditions of the working-class character of Eva Smith/Daisy Renton[4].

[2] AO2: paragraph shows how Priestley's set description helps to establish his ideas.

[3] AO3: clear link to the play's context and message.

The Inspector's arrival also symbolises the dismantling of the Birlings' view of themselves. This idea is emphasised using stage lighting, which moves from 'pink and intimate' to being 'brighter and harder' as the Inspector begins his questioning[4]. This creates an intense atmosphere as the family's secrets and hypocrisies are revealed, the change in lighting symbolising the Inspector's search for the truth[5].

[4] AO2: well selected details, linking different dramatic techniques.

[5] AO1: perceptive focus on how setting and stagecraft help *tell* the story and convey particular ideas.

Props are also used throughout the Inspector's interrogation to help Priestley undermine the Birlings[5]. For example, the photograph of Eva is used to physically connect the characters to their actions: as they hold the photograph and react to it, the audience witnesses their varying levels of guilt and responsibility. This tangible representation of Eva/Daisy adds emotional weight to the narrative: while she is not physically on stage, the Inspector forces the Birlings to look at her during his interrogation[5].

Stage directions add another dimension to the rising <u>dramatic tension</u>[6]. Throughout the play, Priestley uses <u>adjectives and **adverbial** phrases</u>[6] to hint at hidden divisions beneath the Birlings' comfortable façade. Lines are delivered '*gaily*' and '*smiling*'; Sheila speaks to Gerald with '*mock aggressiveness*' as she makes jokes about his faithfulness[6]. On being informed of Eva's violent suicide, Mr Birling responds '*impatiently*'[6] to the Inspector's questions; Sheila is immediately '*rather distressed*'[6] and Eric replies '*involuntarily*'[6] with an exclamation of shock. <u>There is a clear distinction made here between the responses of the more empathetic younger characters and their parents</u>[7]. Like her husband, Mrs Birling refuses to accept responsibility and attempts to answer 'with dignity' as she tries to justify her actions. Gerald, a more ambivalent character, responds to questions 'hesitantly' as he thinks through the consequences of his answers. <u>By the play's end there is another noticeable shift in stage directions as the Birlings become increasingly powerless</u>[7]. When the Inspector leaves after delivering his final speech, the family are left '*staring, subdued and wondering*', and by the close of Act Three, they are left staring '*guiltily and dumbfounded*' as the curtain falls.

<u>In conclusion, Priestley combines setting, props and stage directions to create a sense of how the Birling family's comfortable existence – and the values they represent – is turned upside down. In a famous production of the play, the set explodes at the end of the final act, with the Birlings' opulent dining room collapsing in front of the audience. This is a fitting metaphor for Priestley's political message regarding the upper classes</u>[8].

[6] AO2: appropriate terminology and well selected details are embedded clearly into the analysis.

[7] AO2: Simple comparisons helps the student focus on the impact of the play's structure.

[8] AO1: conclusion neatly summarises the overall effect of setting and stagecraft, using further reading about the play and performance.

Commentary
This is a challenging question, and the student successfully covers a lot of ground. It is an exploratory and thoughtful essay that is based on a strong central idea: the set itself represents the values Priestley wishes to condemn and overthrow, and the student considers how different aspects of stagecraft combine to create this overall effect. The examples used are varied and precisely illustrated and show a sophisticated understanding of how the play operates in performance.

DO IT!

Now use what you've learned to answer the following AQA exam-style question.

How does Priestley change the audience's impression of the Birling family over the course of *An Inspector Calls*?

Write about:

- how Priestley establishes our first impression of the Birling family through the way he writes
- how and why this changes through the play.

[30 marks]

Question 8

How does Priestley explore ideas about family life in *An Inspector Calls*?

Write about:

- how Priestley writes about family life

- what Priestley wants the audience to think about families and their role in society.

[30 marks]

Zoom in on the question

How does Priestley explore ideas about family life in *An Inspector Calls*?

Write about:
- how Priestley writes about family life
- what Priestley wants the audience to think about families and their role in society.

Analyse the role of the family in the play and the lives of the characters. (AO1)

Select relevant details from the play that shape the audience's response. (AO2)

Consider how the presentation of family life links to the play's historical context and Priestley's political views. (AO3)

Here are some ideas that could be included in an answer to this question which covers the Assessment Objectives (AOs):

AO1
Social status and ambition: how the Birlings' desire to climb the social ladder impacts their family dynamics.
Generation gap: the different values of younger and older family members. The play was first performed in 1946 and is set in 1912; the family values represent those of a previous generation.
Superficial appearances: the Inspector's interrogation reveals hidden secrets in the family.
The family appears as a dysfunctional unit that restricts individual thought and human relationships.

AO2
Consider how the characters speak and act towards each other.
Act One: Eric challenges Mr Birling's values.
Gerald and Sheila's wedding arrangements are formal, and marriage is presented as primarily about social advancement.
Men are associated with 'work' and 'business'; women are expected to follow their husband's wishes.
The end of the play: Eric and Sheila reject their parents' values and hypocrisy.

AO3
The family unit as a **microcosm** for a patriarchal society based on strict expectations: parents and children, men and women, are expected to act in clearly defined ways.
Family life affects people's behaviour and ensures the same values are passed on from generation to generation.
Priestley's negative portrayal of upper-class family life connects to his political ideas.

A student has decided to write an essay that argues that Priestley's presentation of family life is linked to his criticism of social class. This is the plan they have made to answer the question.

Paragraph	Content		Timing
1	Introduction – Priestley examines family life through the Birlings. He is mostly critical of them and the type of family relationships they represent.	Explain how Priestley's presentation of family life links to his criticism of social class.	9.35
2	Marriage – The Birling family connections prioritise appearance and social status over love. The house is 'substantial and heavily comfortable, but not cosy and homelike.'		9.45
3	Husbands – Upper-class men (e.g. Arthur/Gerald) were expected to be the heads of families and prioritise wealth and social advancement. Mrs Birling to Sheila: 'men with important work to do sometimes have to spend nearly all their time and energy on their business. You'll have to get used to that, just as I had.'	Explain how these relationships are strained and prevent individuals from connecting.	10.00
4	Wives – Upper-class women (e.g. Sheila/ Sybil) were expected to follow their men and support their ambitions. Mrs Birling: 'I think Sheila and I had better go into the drawing room and leave you men.'		10.05
5	Children – Expected to be respectful of their elders and not think for themselves (Sheila and Eric).		10.10
6	Conclusion – The Inspector and Eva/Daisy's story highlights the hypocrisy behind the Birling family's façade. The Birling family is a microcosm of broader social problems.		10.15

The essay plan above will meet these Assessment Objectives:

AO1 Read, understand and respond	Breaks the question focus down into different areas for analysis. Outlines a key conceptual answer.
AO2 Language, form and structure	Offers a broad range of examples from across the text. Allows for close analysis of key scenes.
AO3 Contexts	Considers how contemporary social values are reflected in the play. Considers how Priestley's political intentions are reflected in the play.

Notice...
The student's answer to this question doesn't just address family life as a single idea. Instead, they structure each point around a different relationship or role within the family unit, which gives their response a coherent structure.

An Inspector Calls focuses on an upper-class family: the Birlings, who have gathered to celebrate the engagement of their daughter Sheila. Priestley presents a largely critical examination of the family unit, inviting the audience to reflect on its significance and broader role in society[1]. The play was written in the mid-1940s but is set in 1912. This allows Priestley to analyse family life from a distance, reflecting on the values of the previous generation.

One of the first things we learn about the Birling family is that they are overly materialistic. This is indicated in the opening stage directions, which describe the Birlings' home as 'substantial and heavily comfortable, but not cosy and homelike.'[2]

It Is also clear from the opening scene that the Birling family is a patriarchal household, in which women are expected to defer to their husbands and fathers[3]. Act One is dominated by Mr Birling, who insists on giving a speech about Sheila's marriage, which he presents almost as a contract between himself and Gerald's aristocratic father – his 'friendly rival' in business. The engagement is, to him, not about love but an opportunity for the two companies to work together 'for lower costs and higher prices.' When any member of his family attempts to interrupt or offer their own views, Mr Birling ignores or dismisses them[4]. In the context of the early 20th century society, marriages were often defined less by love than considerations of social class and financial security[5].

The lack of personal connection within the Edwardian family is further explored when the female characters leave the dinner party to allow the men to discuss politics and business. Mr Birling tries to impress Gerald with his forthcoming knighthood; they joke about their 'nice well-behaved family' being caught in a scandal and laugh 'complacently'[6]. This formal separation of the sexes was common in Edwardian Britain, and the play demonstrates how upper-class men were seen as 'heads' of the family and used marriage as a means of forming alliances, consolidating their wealth and power[7]. In contrast, the female characters are expected to follow their husband's wishes. When Gerald gives Sheila an engagement ring, she asks him, 'excited, 'is it the one you wanted me to have?' – Gerald choosing her ring points to the power imbalance in their relationship. When Shelia

[1] AO1: outlines the areas they will examine and the start of their argument.

[2] AO2: supports ideas with concise evidence from the text.

[3] AO1: develops argument, looking at another element of family life.

[4] AO2: develops analysis, with summary of action combined with relevant details.

[5] AO3: indicates the context in which the play was written.

[6] AO2: further examples given of how the idea develops across the play.

[7] AO3: roots analysis in the context of its setting.

later complains that Gerald has been spending too much time at work, Mrs Birling tells her that men 'spend nearly all their time and energy on their business. You'll have to get used to that.'[8] Furthermore, while Mrs Birling comes from a wealthier background, it is Arthur Birling who has the higher status as her husband. Many productions of the play emphasise this tension, portraying the Birlings' marriage as strained and distant[9].

This lack of emotional connection is also shown in the family's parent–child relationships;[10] as adults, Sheila and Eric refer to their parents as 'Mummy' and 'Father'; yet they are not close.

The Inspector's arrival brings these tensions to the surface, revealing that[11] Sheila is deeply unhappy; Eric has an alcohol problem and has stolen money from the business; Gerald has been sexually unfaithful to Sheila; the Birling family's collective disregard for the well-being of others has led to Eva/Daisy's suicide[12]. These scandalous revelations undermine the family's moral façade as 'respectable citizens'. Rather than being a loving family unit, then, the Birling family appears claustrophobic and emotionally damaged. In this, the Birlings serve as a microcosm for broader society, in which ignorance and inequality are passed from one generation to the next. Hope for the future, Priestley seems to suggest, is found by breaking free from this oppressive family cycle. By the end of the play, Sheila and Eric have matured and rejected their parents' generation, with Sheila telling her parents that they 'are being childish'. By allowing the younger members of the Birling family this escape, Priestley also invites the audience to consider their own understanding of family, empathy and human interconnectedness[13].

8 AO2: makes a successful comparison between characters. Supports ideas with concise, relevant details.

9 AO3: understanding of context of performance.

10 AO1: develops argument by looking at another element of family life.

11 AO1: interesting sub-point on how play develops the theme.

12 AO2: effective summary of events to support point.

13 AO1: a perceptive conclusion which summarises ideas about the family as a social unit and addresses Priestley's intentions as a playwright.

Commentary
This is an intelligent response that demonstrates a perceptive understanding of the play's context and themes. It uses comparisons between different characters and relationships to develop a coherent, conceptual argument about the presentation of family life in *An Inspector Calls*. Relevant supporting details are used throughout and are clearly embedded into the analysis.

DO IT!

Now use what you've learned to answer the following AQA exam-style question.

How does Priestley explore ideas about love in *An Inspector Calls*?

Write about:

- how Priestley explores ideas about love through characters and events in the play
- what Priestley wants the audience to think about love.

[30 marks]

Exam-style question 1

How far does Priestley present Mrs Birling as a character who refuses to learn lessons about herself or change in *An Inspector Calls*?

Write about:

• what Mrs Birling says and does

• how far she refuses to learn lessons or change and why Priestley presents her this way.

[30 marks]

PLANIT!

Answer steps	Content	Key ideas to refer to throughout answer	Minutes per step
Intro/Overall main point			
Sub-point 1			
Sub-point 2			
Sub-point 3			
Conclusion			

Exam-style question 2

How does Priestley explore the gap between different generations in *An Inspector Calls*?

Write about:

- how Priestley presents the gaps between the generations
- why Priestley presents the gaps between generations in this way.

[30 marks]

PLANIT!

Answer steps	Content	Key ideas to refer to throughout answer	Minutes per step
Intro/Overall main point			
Sub-point 1			
Sub-point 2			
Sub-point 3			
Conclusion			

Exam-style question 3

How does Priestley explore ideas of personal and social responsibility in *An Inspector Calls*?

Write about:

- how Priestley explores ideas of personal and social responsibility through the characters and events of the play
- how Priestley wants to audience to respond.

[30 marks]

PLANIT!

Answer steps	Content	Key ideas to refer to throughout answer	Minutes per step
Intro/Overall main point			
Sub-point 1			
Sub-point 2			
Sub-point 3			
Conclusion			

Exam-style question 4

To what extent can Gerald be considered a 'villain' in *An Inspector Calls*?

Write about:

- what Gerald says and does throughout the play
- how far he can be considered a villain.

[30 marks]

PLANIT!

Answer steps	Content	Key ideas to refer to throughout answer	Minutes per step
Intro/Overall main point			
Sub-point 1			
Sub-point 2			
Sub-point 3			
Conclusion			

Exam-style question 5

'*An Inspector Calls* leaves too many questions unanswered at the end of Act Three to be satisfying.'

To what extent do you agree with this view of the ending of the play?

Write about:

• how Priestley ends the play in Act Three

• the extent to which the ending can be considered satisfying for the audience.

[30 marks]

PLANIT!

Answer steps	Content	Key ideas to refer to throughout answer	Minutes per step
Intro/Overall main point			
Sub-point 1			
Sub-point 2			
Sub-point 3			
Conclusion			

Exam-style question 6

How does Priestley explore ideas about gender and inequality in *An Inspector Calls*?

Write about:

- how Priestley explores gender and inequality through events in the play
- how the audience might respond to these ideas.

[30 marks]

PLANIT!

Answer steps	Content	Key ideas to refer to throughout answer	Minutes per step
Intro/Overall main point			
Sub-point 1			
Sub-point 2			
Sub-point 3			
Conclusion			

How does Priestley explore ideas about social class in *An Inspector Calls*?

Write about:

- how Priestley explores ideas about social class through the characters and events of the play
- how the audience might respond to these ideas.

[30 marks]

PLANIT!

Answer steps	Content	Key ideas to refer to throughout answer	Minutes per step
Intro/Overall main point			
Sub-point 1			
Sub-point 2			
Sub-point 3			
Conclusion			

Exam-style question 8

'I'm talking as a hard-headed, practical man of business.' (Mr Birling, Act One)

How does Priestley use Mr Birling to explore ideas about obtaining wealth and caring for other people in *An Inspector Calls*?

Write about:

- how Mr Birling speaks about wealth and caring for other people
- how he contrasts with other characters in the play and why Priestley presents him this way.

[30 marks]

PLANIT!

Answer steps	Content	Key ideas to refer to throughout answer	Minutes per step
Intro/Overall main point			
Sub-point 1			
Sub-point 2			
Sub-point 3			
Conclusion			

Glossary

adjective Word that describes a noun (for example, *brown* eyes).

adverbial Word or phrase expressing manner (for example, excitedly, hesitatingly).

atmosphere The overall mood of a scene in a fiction or drama (for example, gloomy, joyous).

catalyst A person or action that starts or speeds up a chain of events (for example, the Inspector).

character A person in a play or story: a person created by the writer (for example: The Inspector, Mr Birling or Daisy/Eva).

context The circumstances in which literature is set, written and read. For *An Inspector Calls*, this could mean the context of 1912, when the play was set, or 1946, when the play was written and first performed, or the current day.

declaratives Sentences in the form of statements that create a tone of certainty (for example, 'There is no chance of war').

dramatic irony When the audience is aware of something of which the characters aren't aware of.

dysphemism/dysphemistic Use of a deliberately shocking or forceful word or phrase rather than a softer alternative (see also **euphemism**).

effect The impact that a writer's word choices or events have on a reader or audience (for example, shock, anticipation, relief).

euphemism/euphemistic Use of a softened word or phrase instead of a harsh, direct one (for example, 'passed on' instead of 'died'); often used as a way of confronting an unpleasant event or idea (see also **dysphemism**).

foreshadowing A method by which an author places clues about an event later in the text.

language The words and the style that a writer chooses in order to have an **effect** on a reader or viewer.

metaphor Comparing two things by referring to them as though they are the same thing.

microcosm A community, place or situation regarded as encapsulating something much larger (for example, 'The Birling family's dining room is a microcosm of the divisions in Edwardian society').

plot The story of the play: the sequence of the events and how they link together.

polemicist Person who engages in passionate debate.

prop Object used on stage or on screen during a dramatic performance.

symbol/symbolism/symbolise The use of a physical object to represent an abstract idea.

stagecraft The technical aspects of theatrical performance, including set design, lighting, props, make-up and costume.

stage directions Descriptions and instructions in a script to guide actors, designers and directors during a theatrical production.

tension/dramatic tension The anticipation that something is about to happen or be revealed in the storyline. Building dramatic tension is the main way writers maintain the audience's attention.

three unities The idea that a play should have one main action, take place in one location and should take place over one point in time (no more than 24 hours).

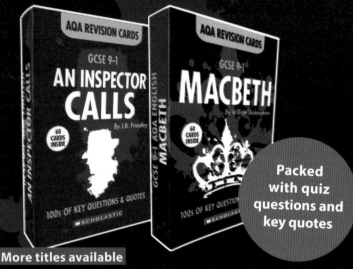
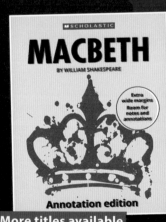

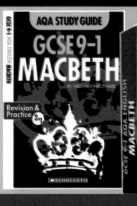